Shut Up & Colour This Shit:
A Swear Word Adult Colouring Book

Georgina Townsend

Shut Up & Colour This Shit: A Swear Word Adult Colouring Book
Edited by Georgina Townsend

Published by Ravensforge Books

ISBN: 978-1-912325-03-0

THIS IS A TEST PAGE, PLEASE FEEL FREE TO TRY OUT YOUR MATERIALS

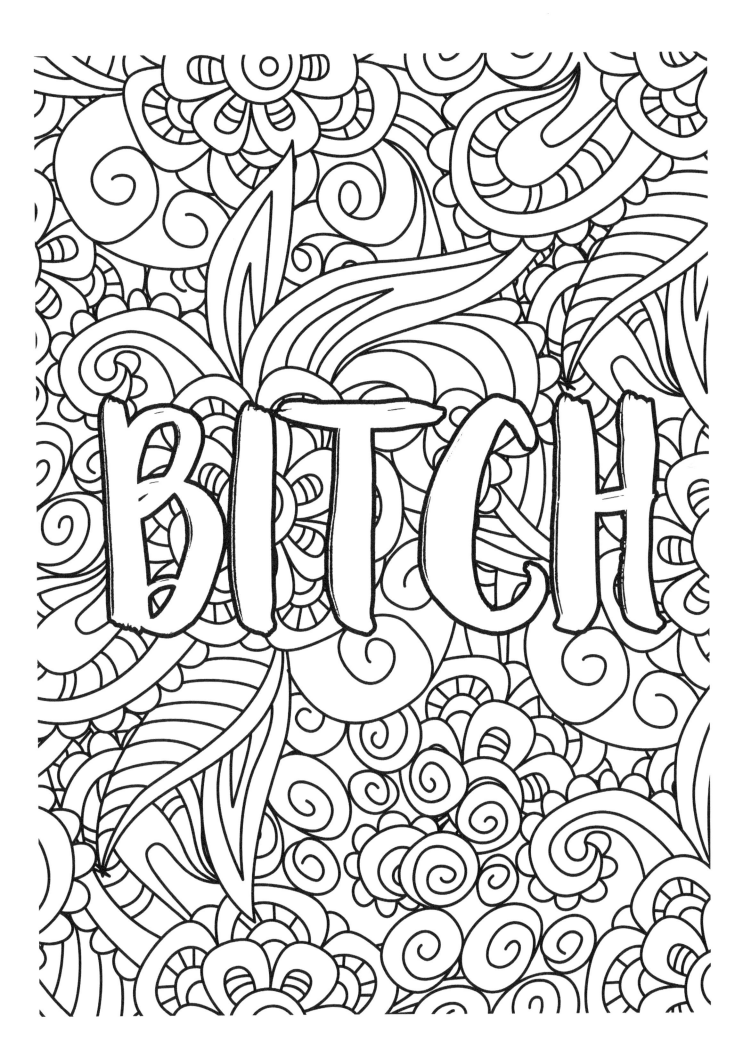

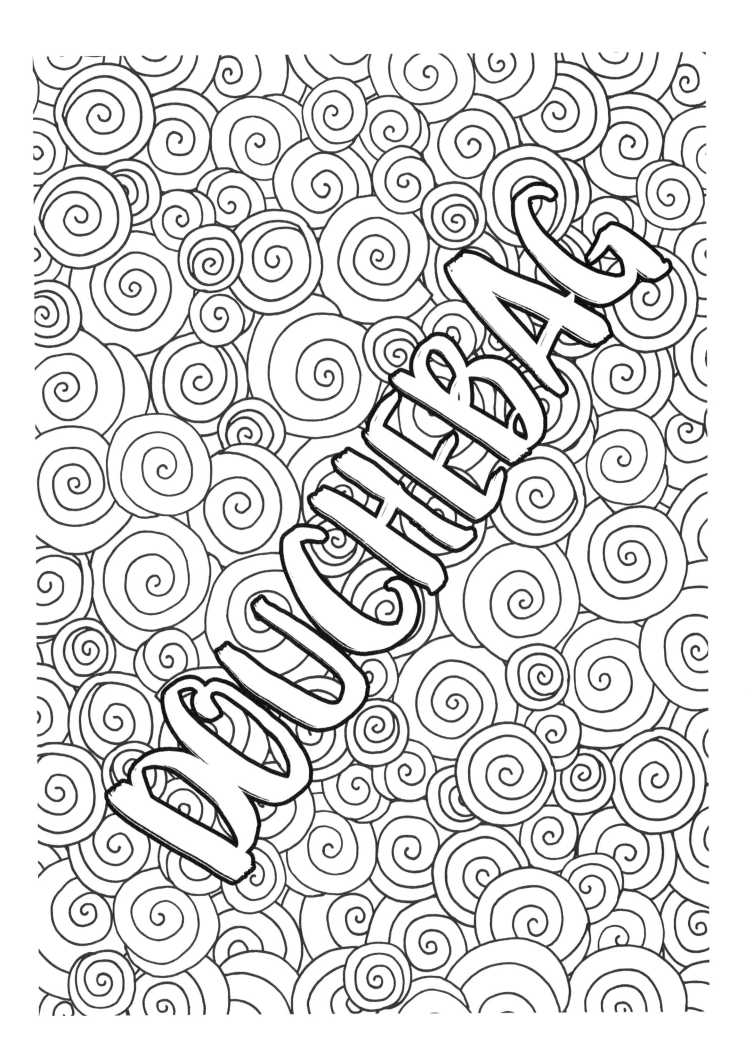

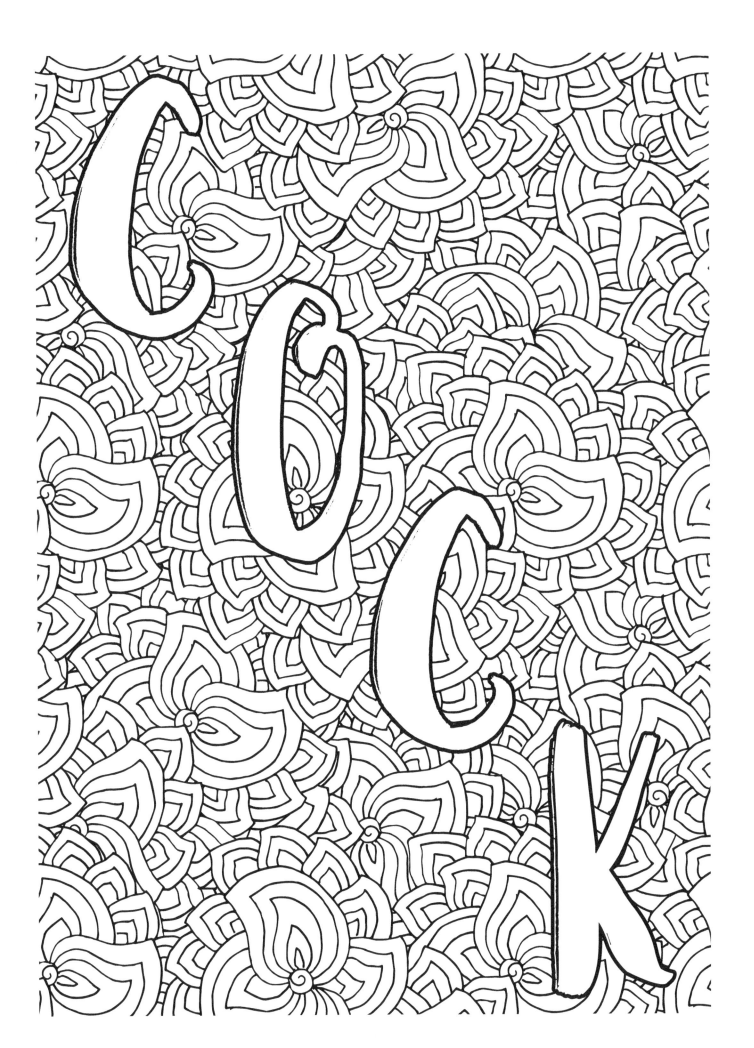

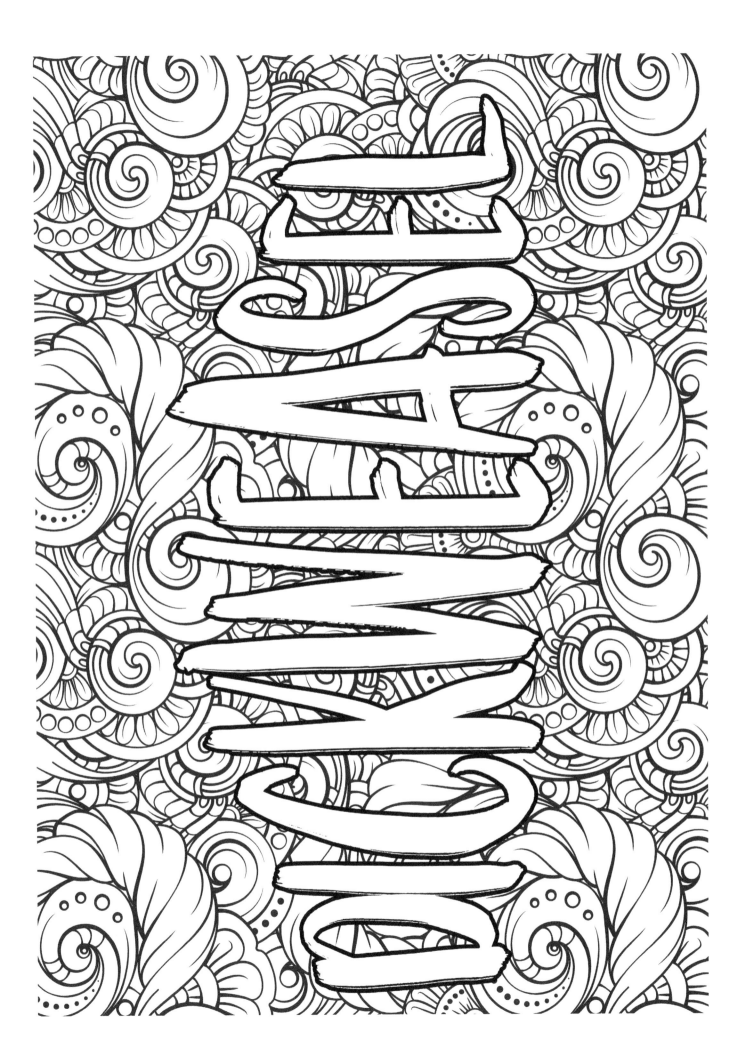

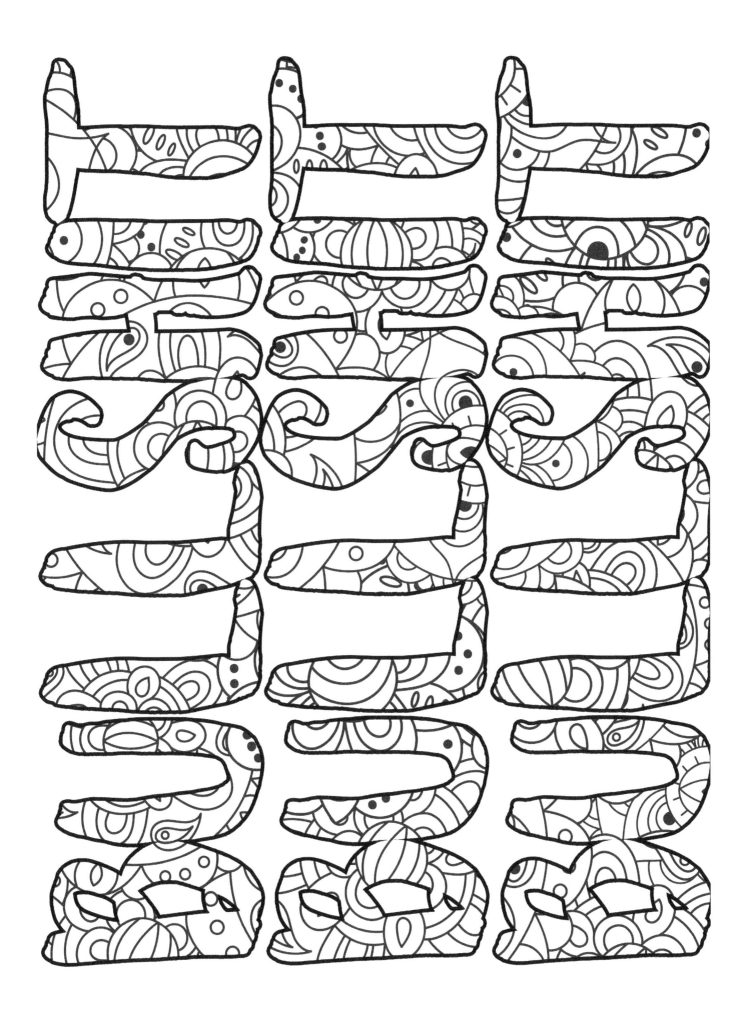

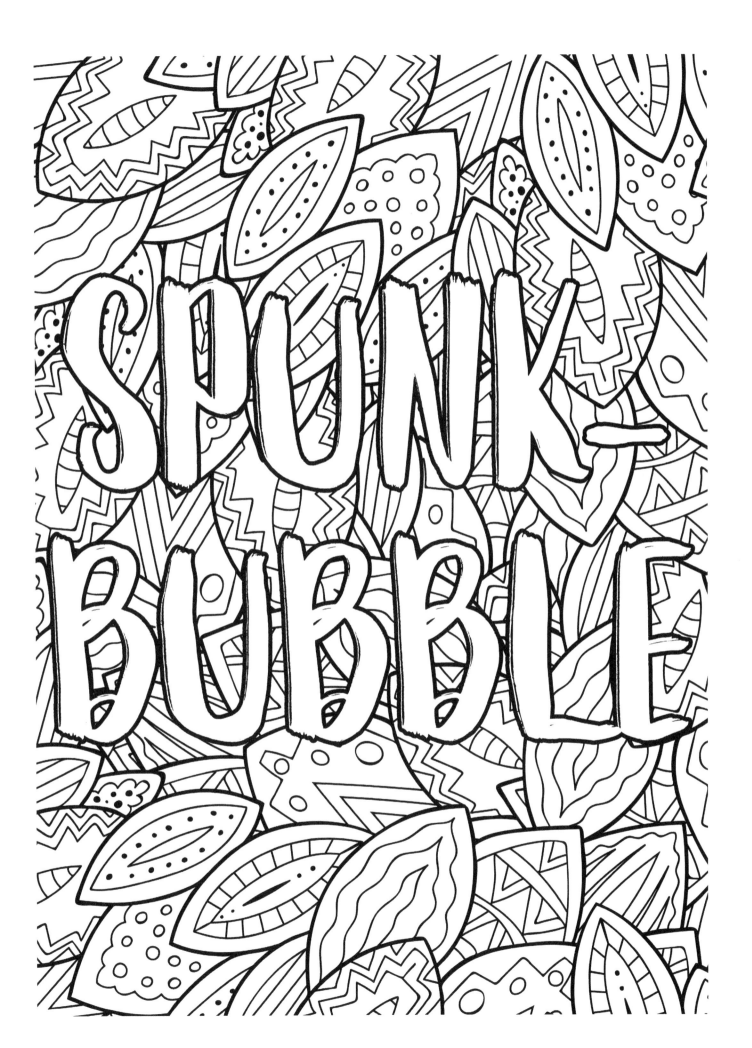

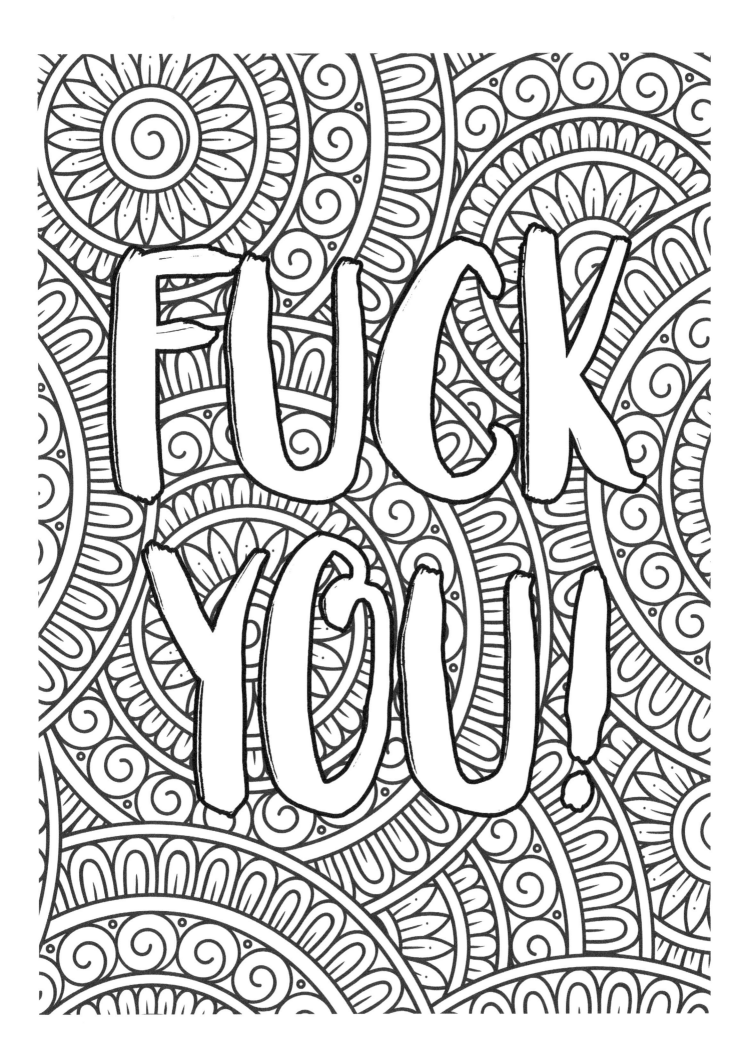

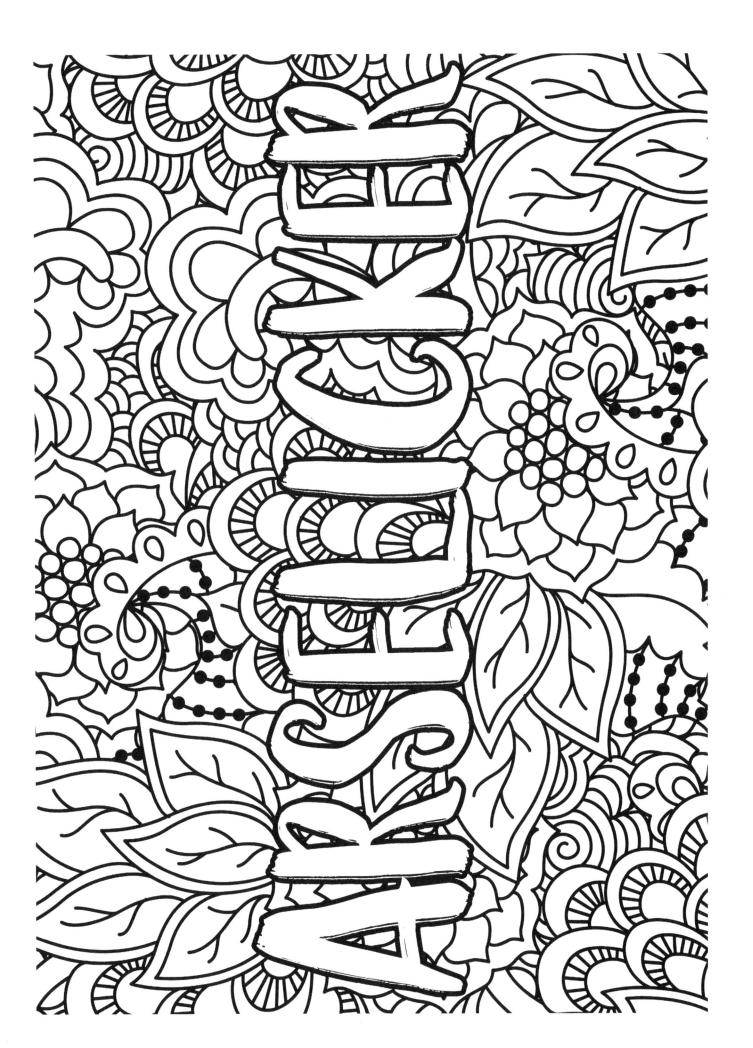

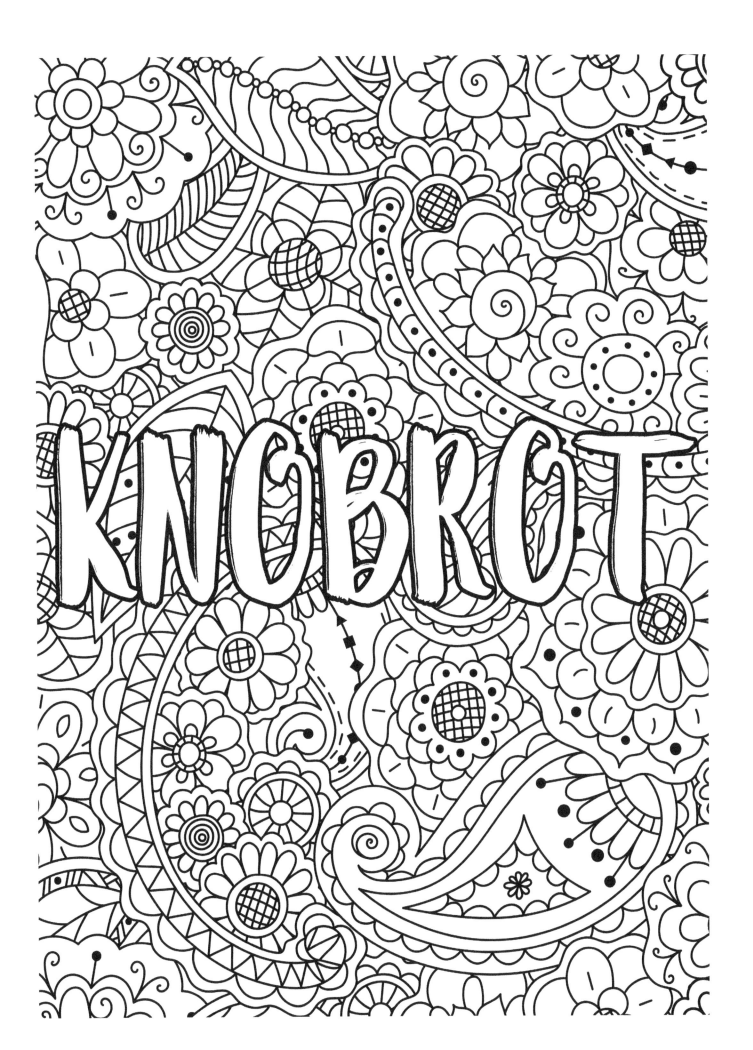

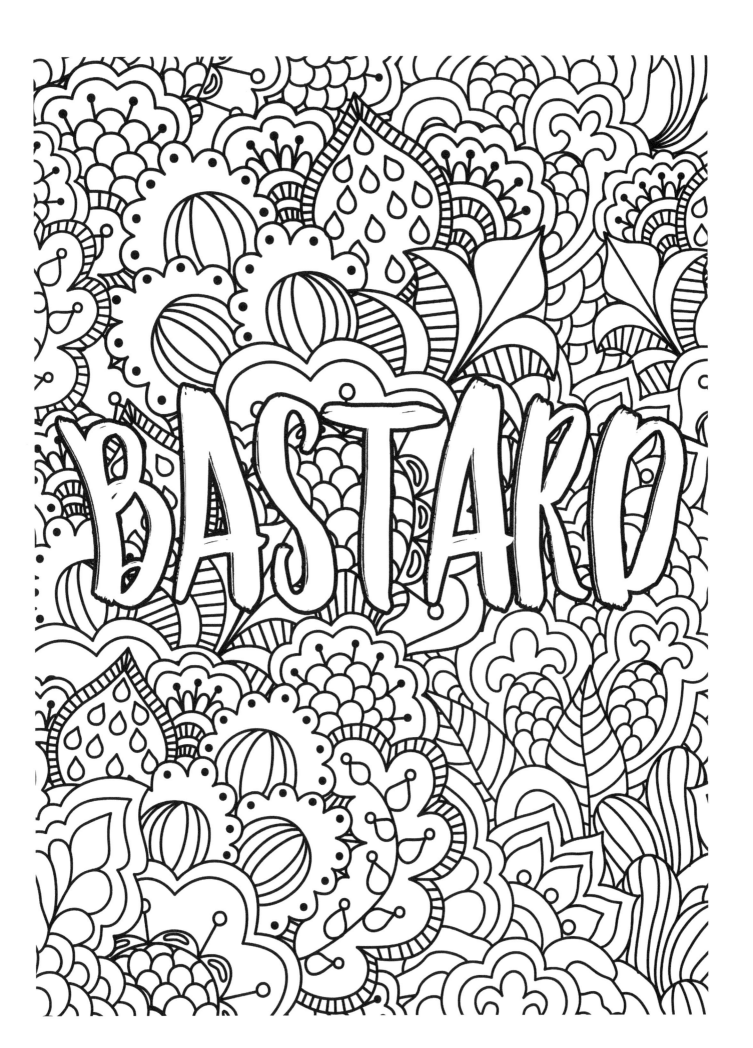

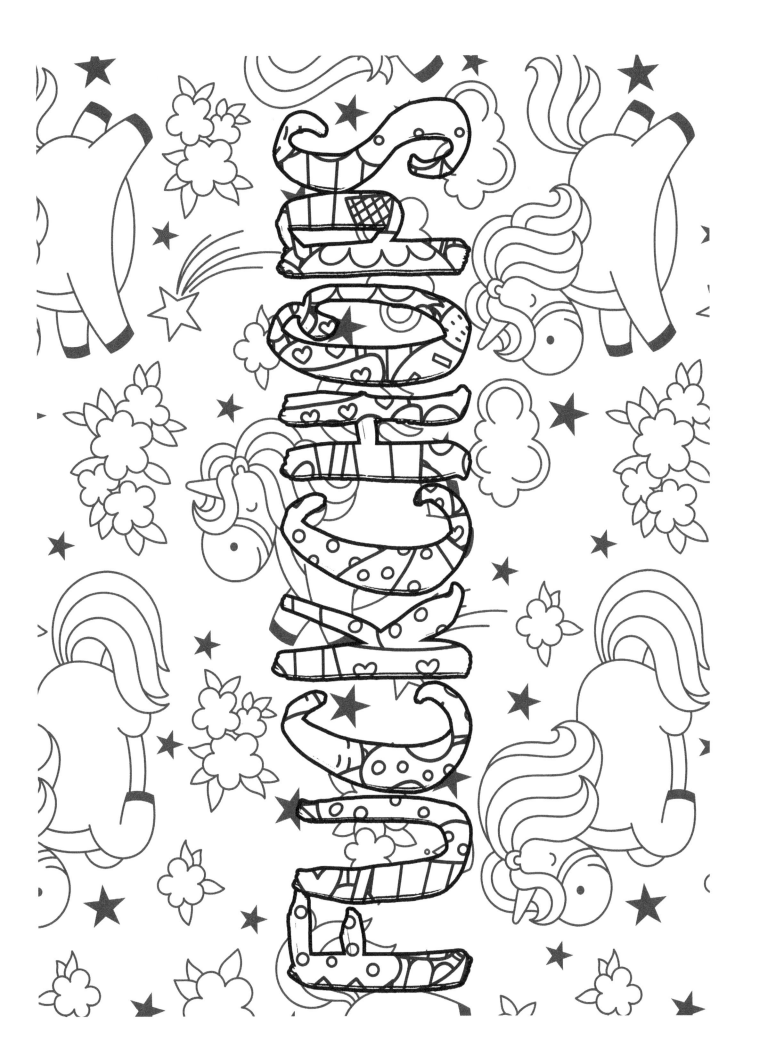

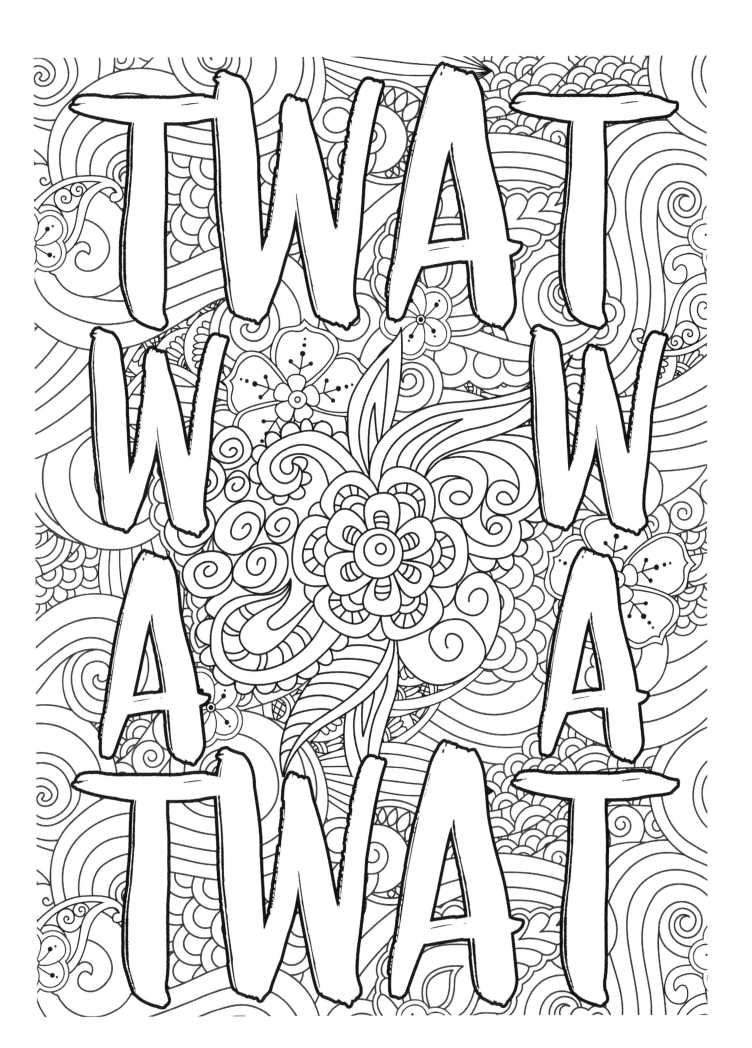

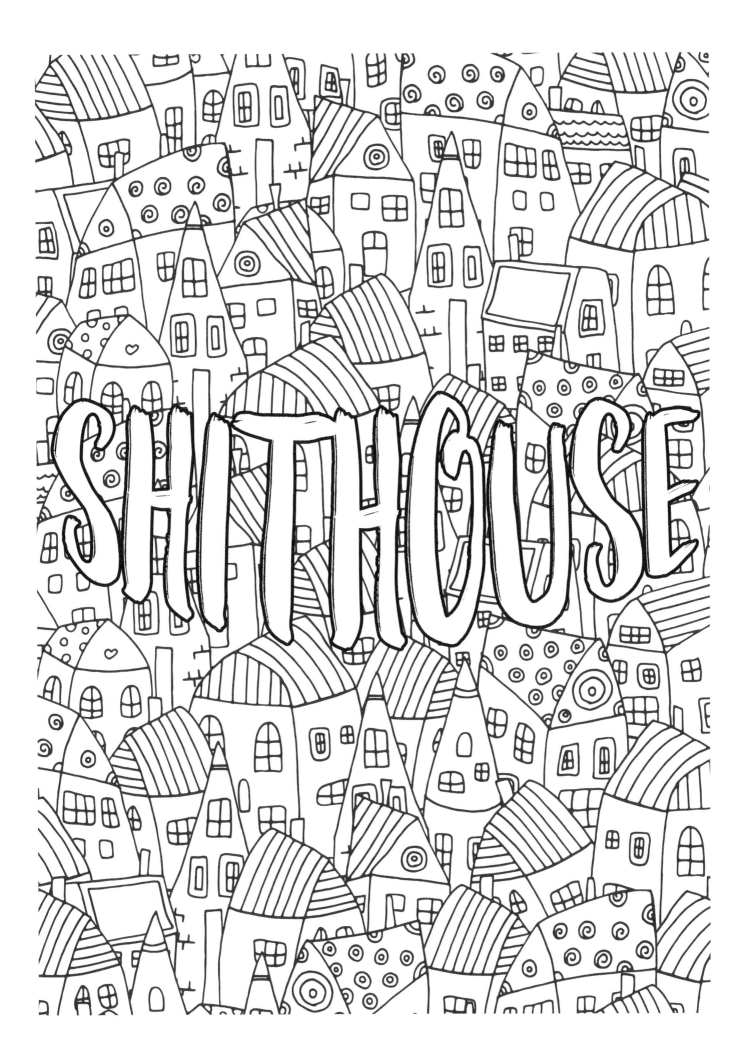

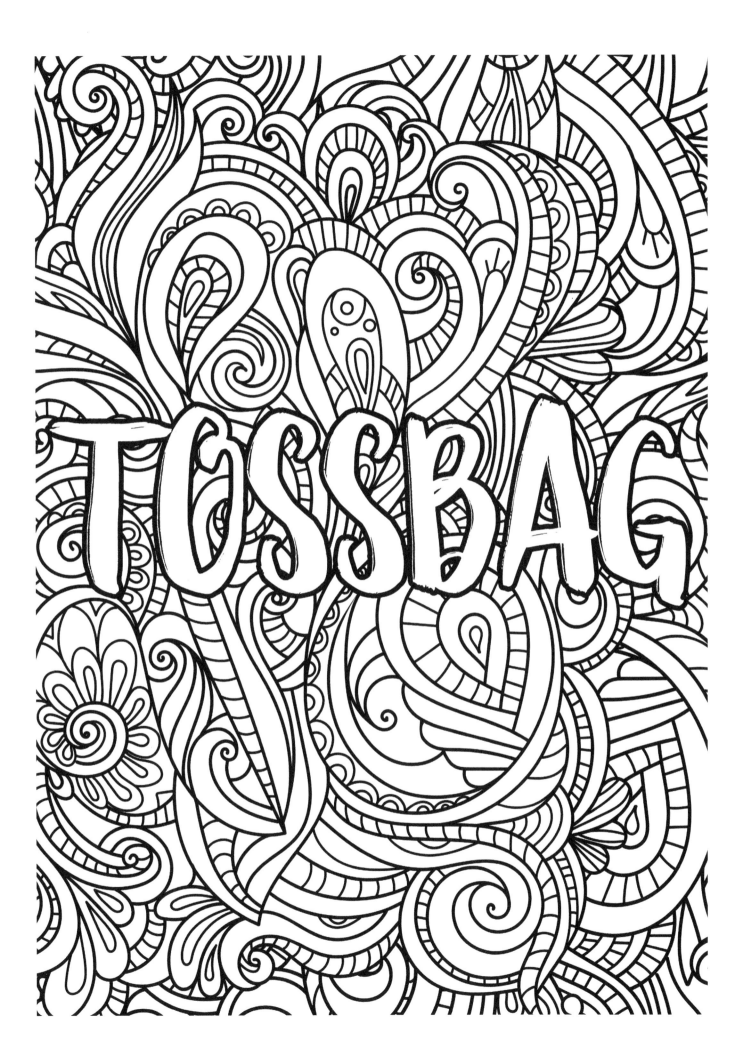

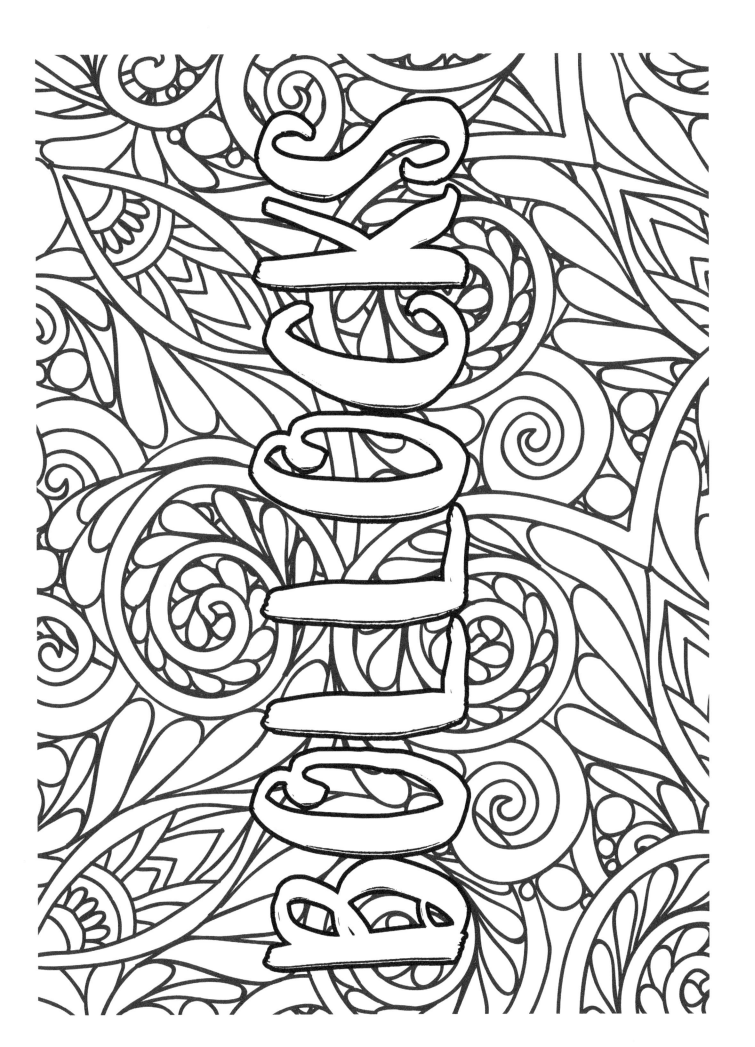

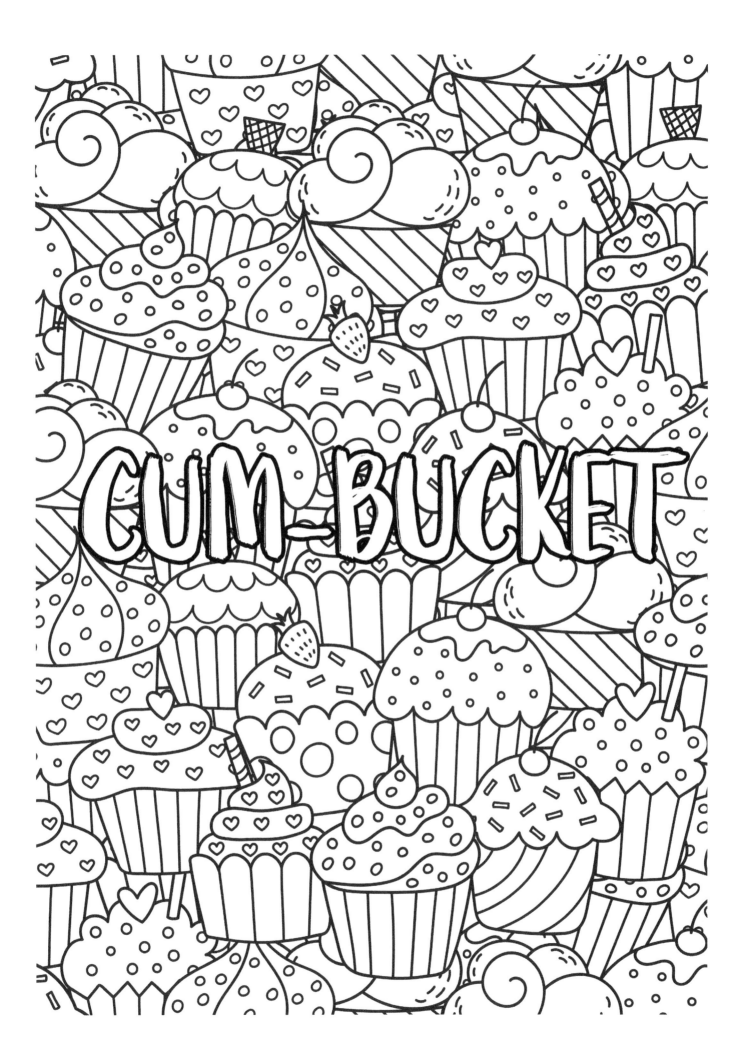

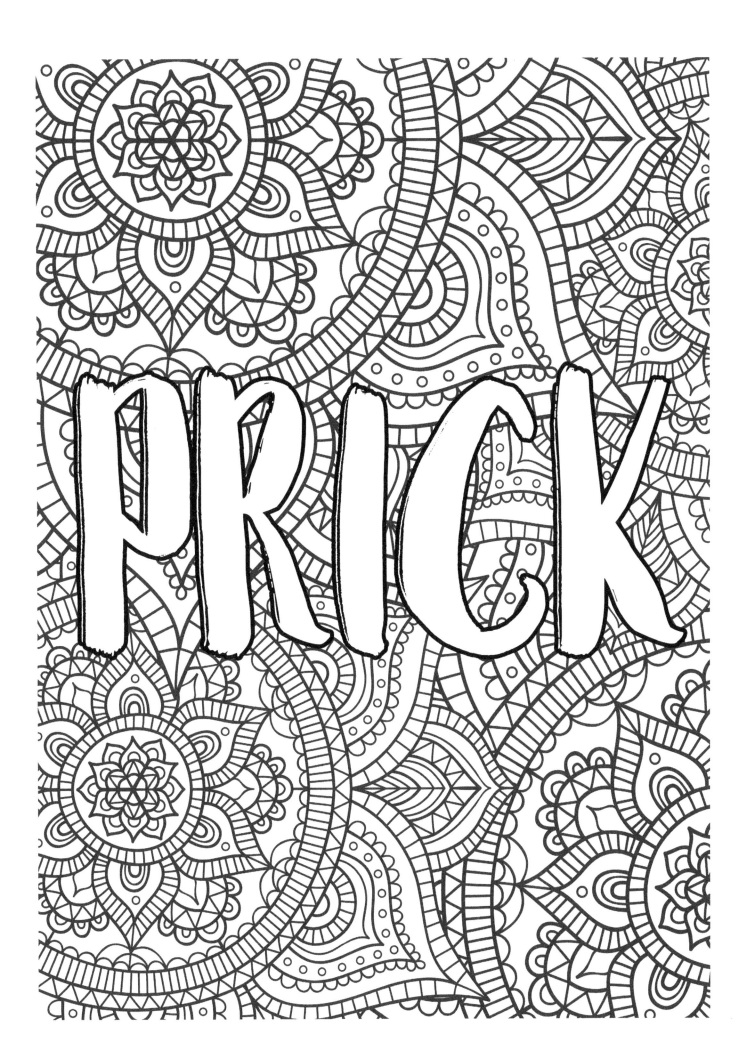

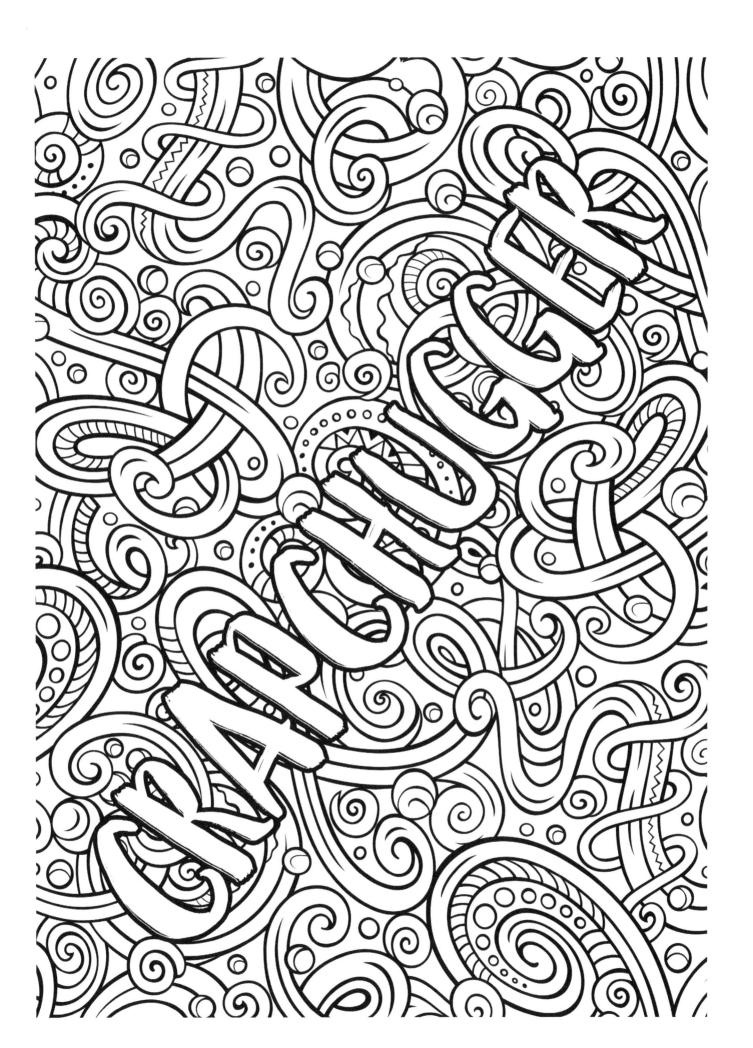

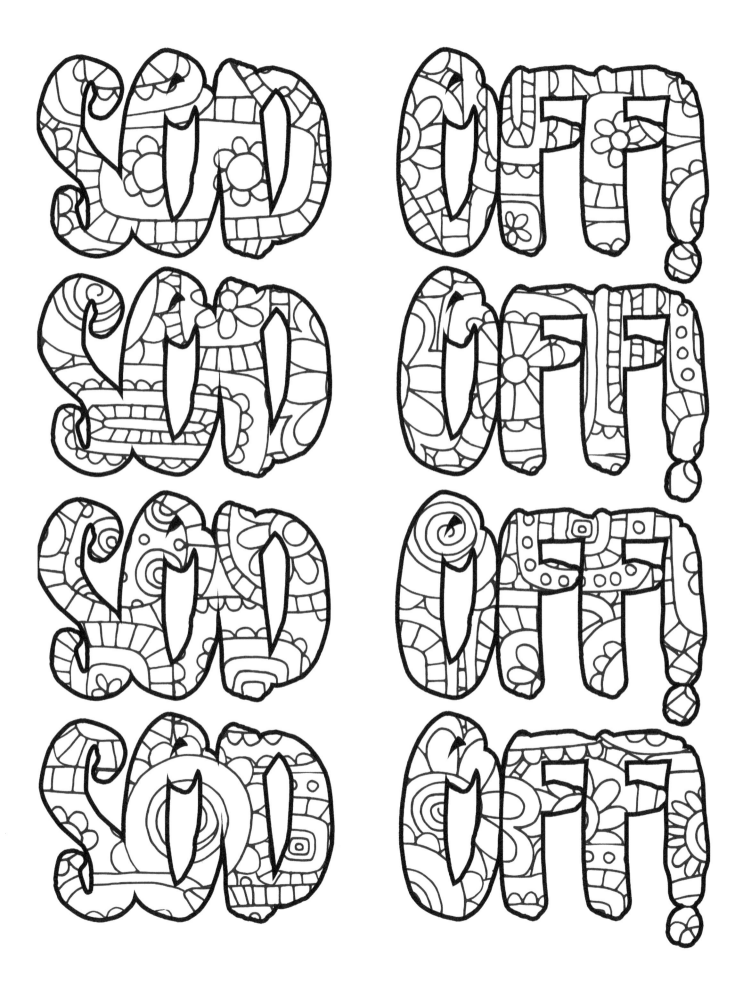

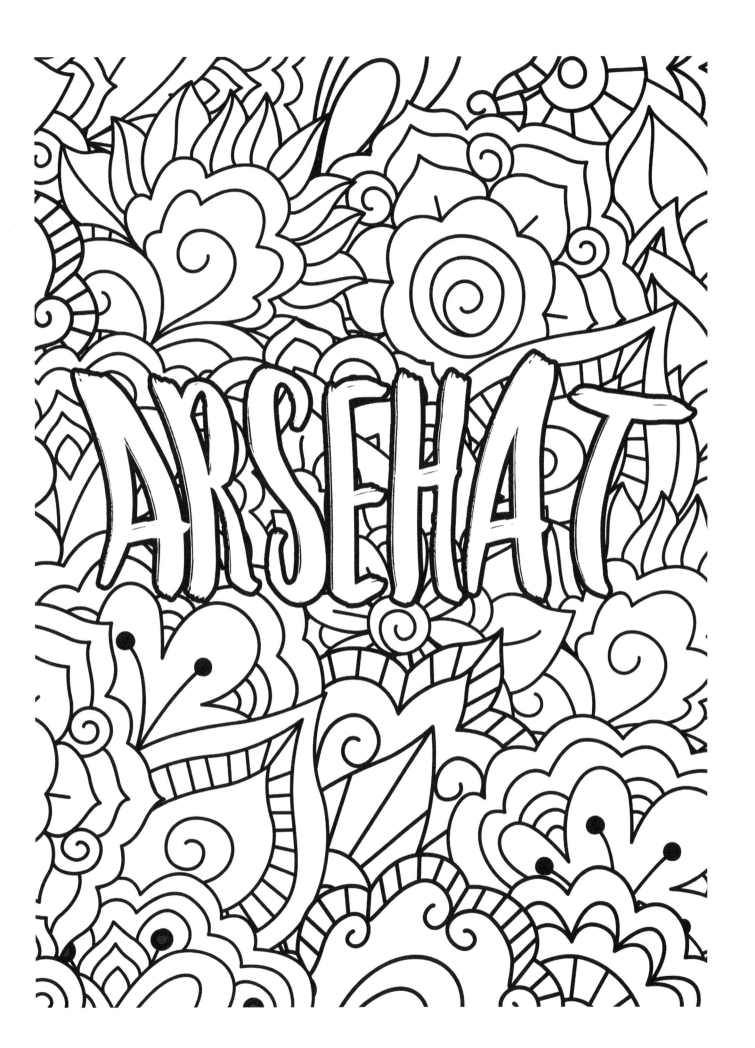

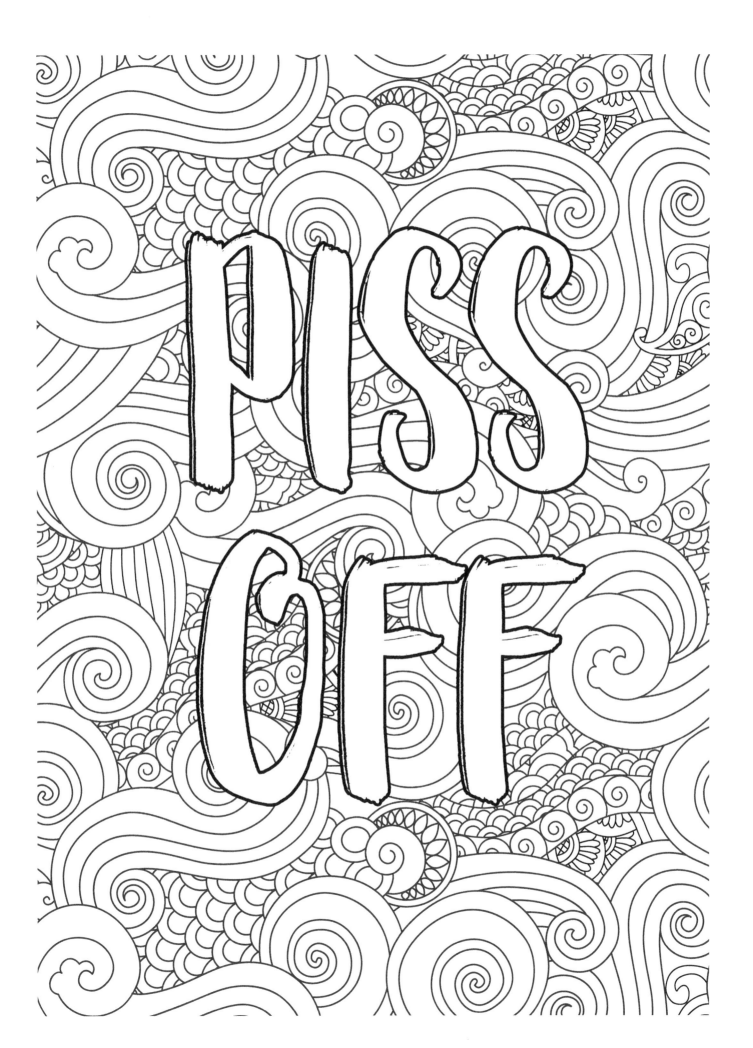

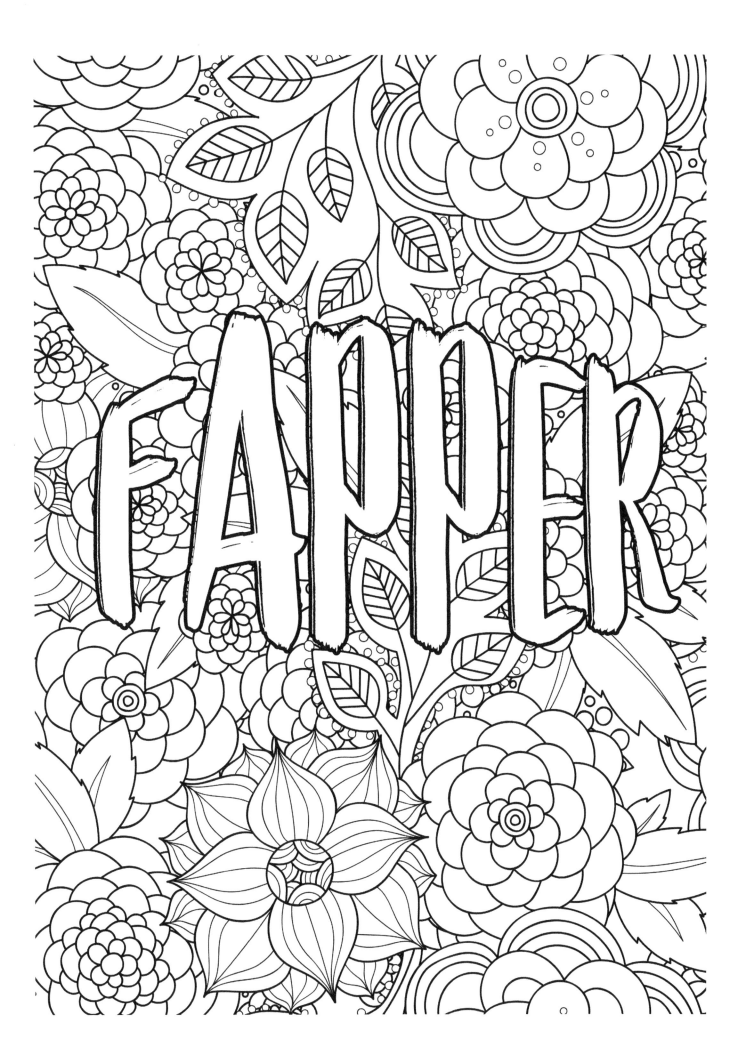

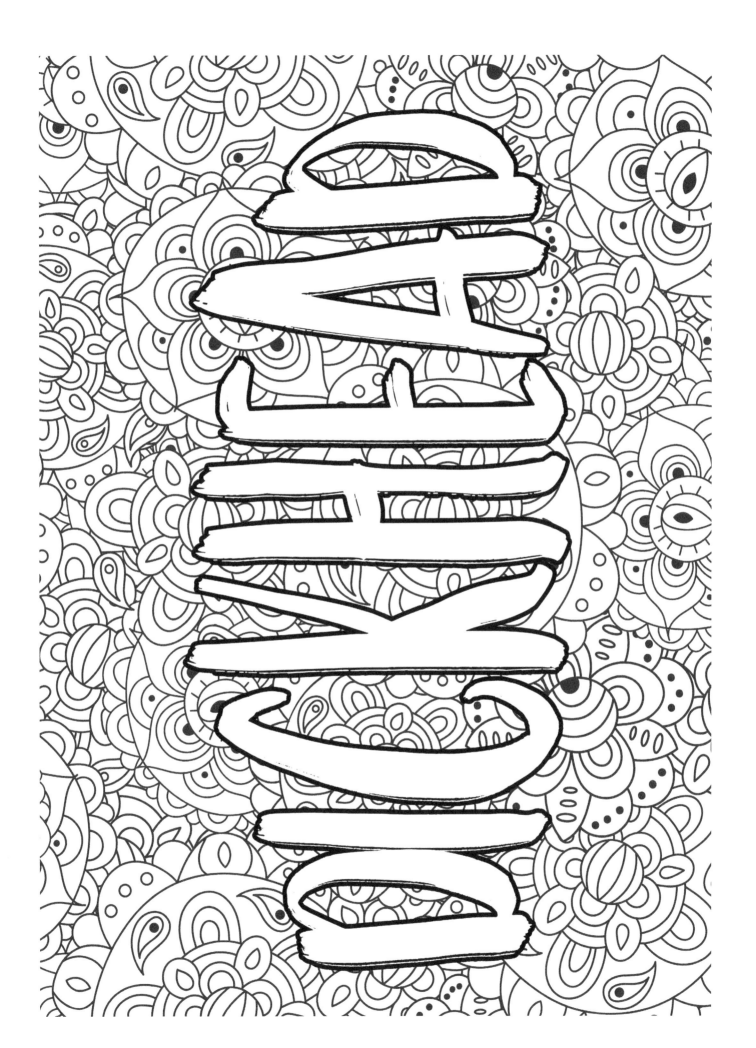

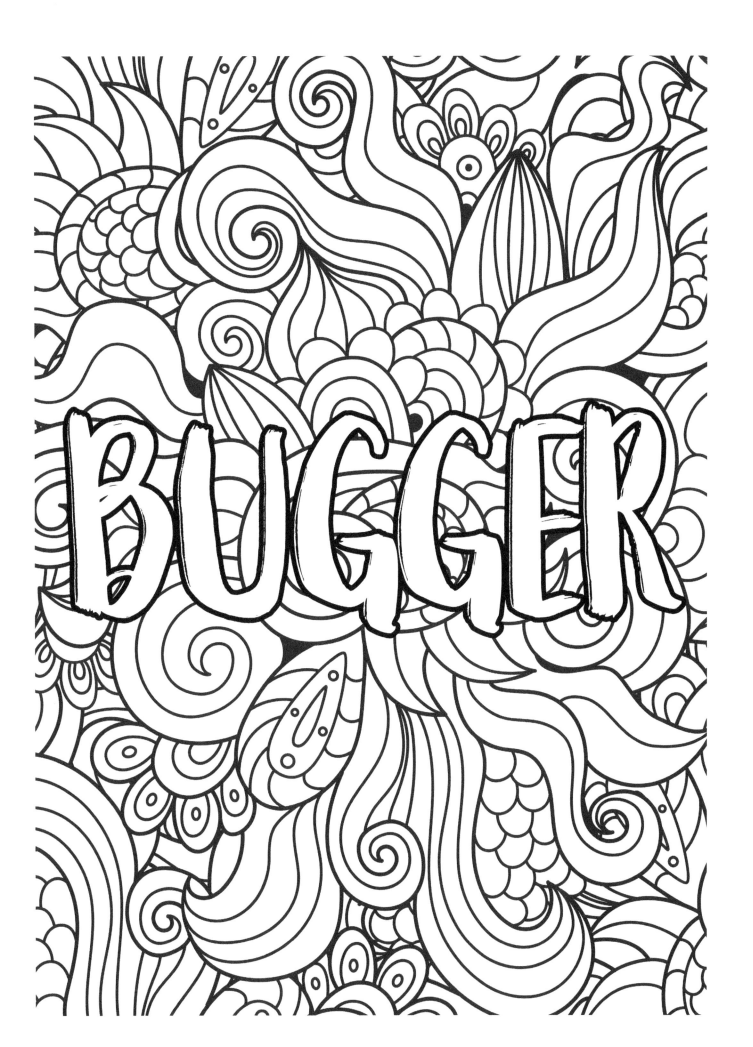

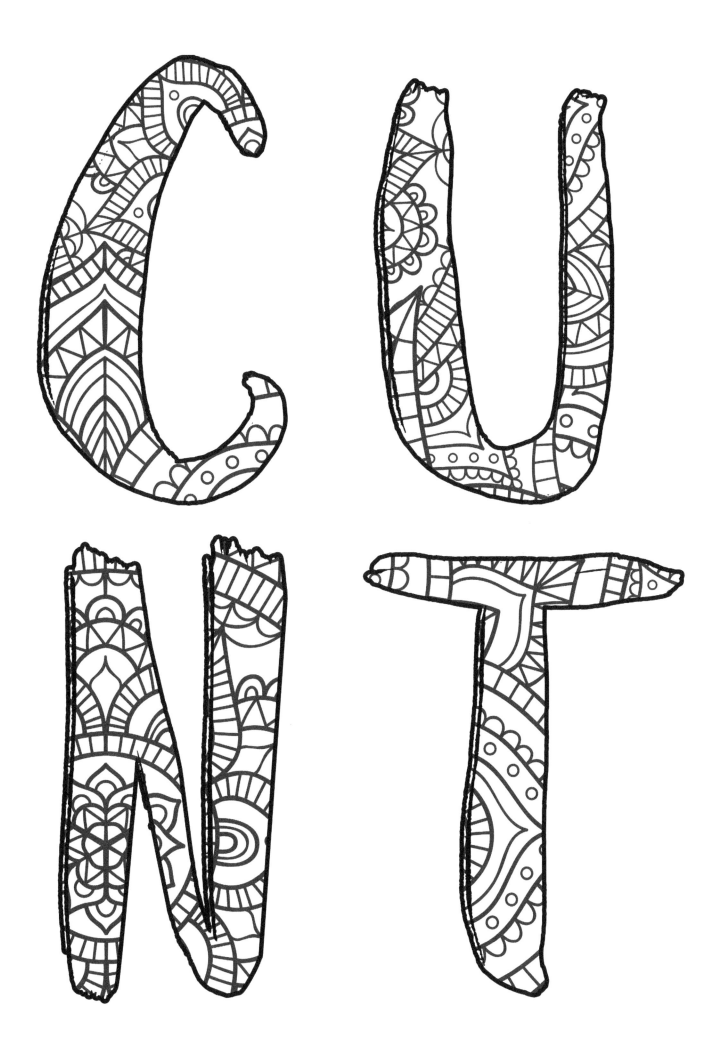

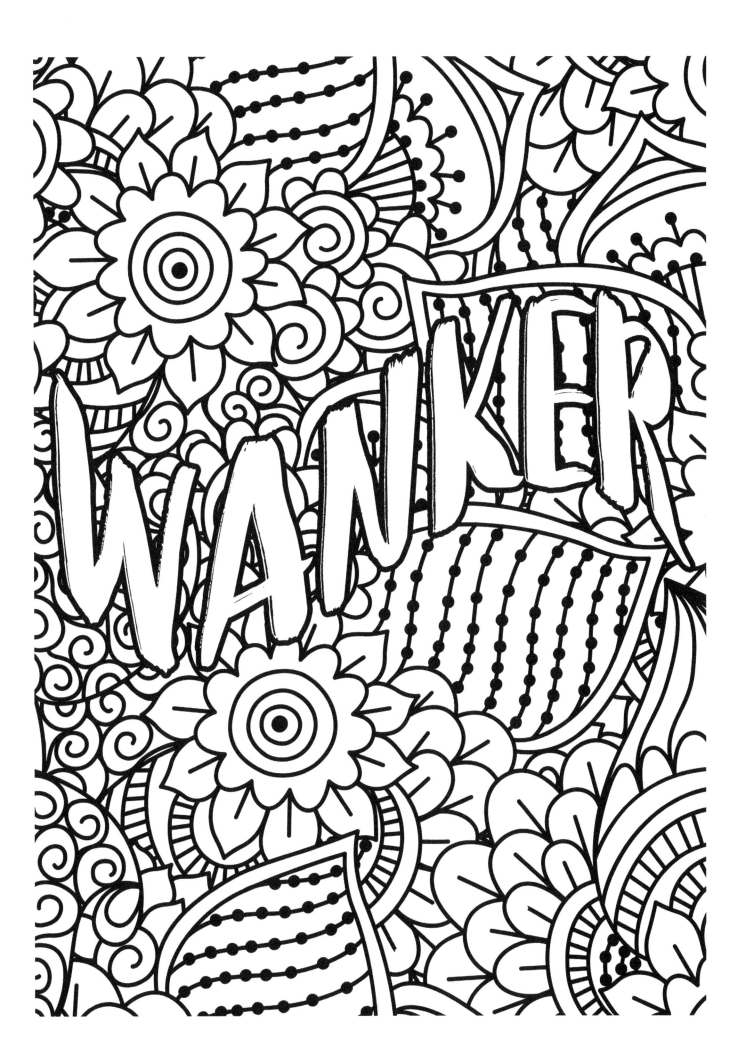

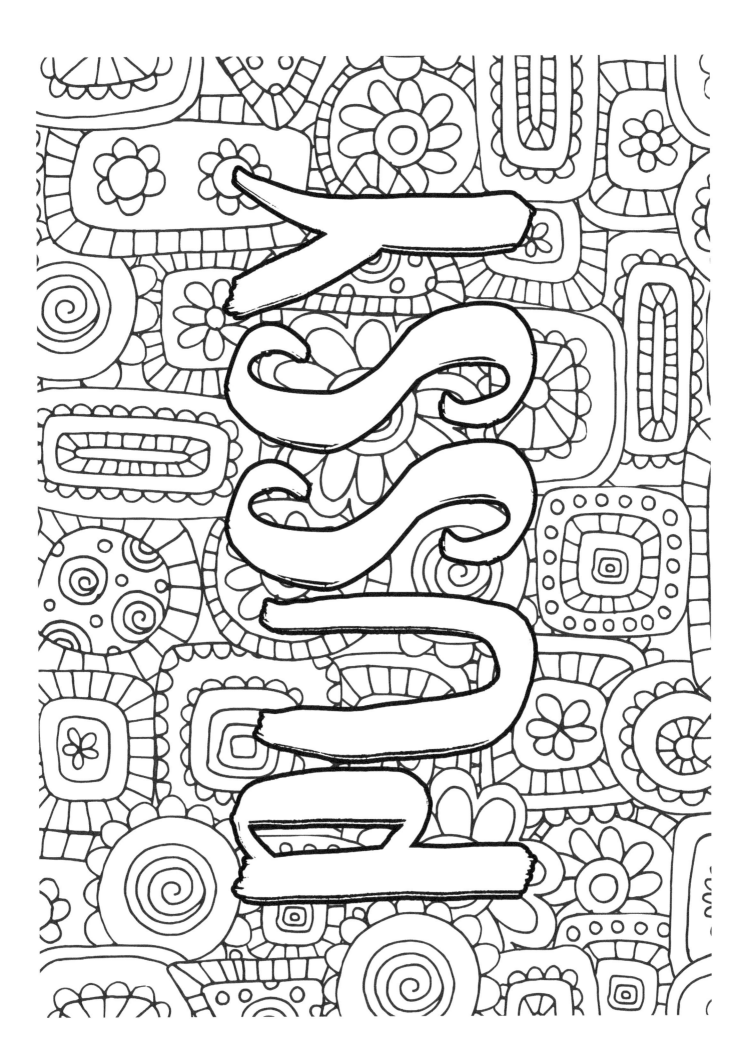

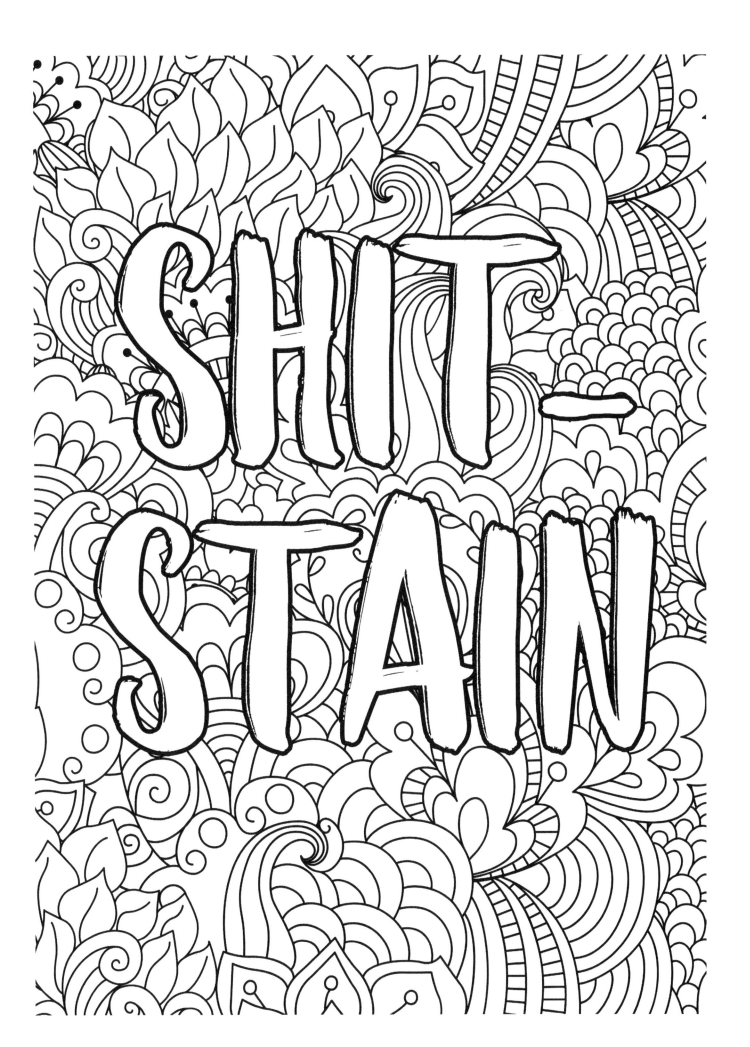

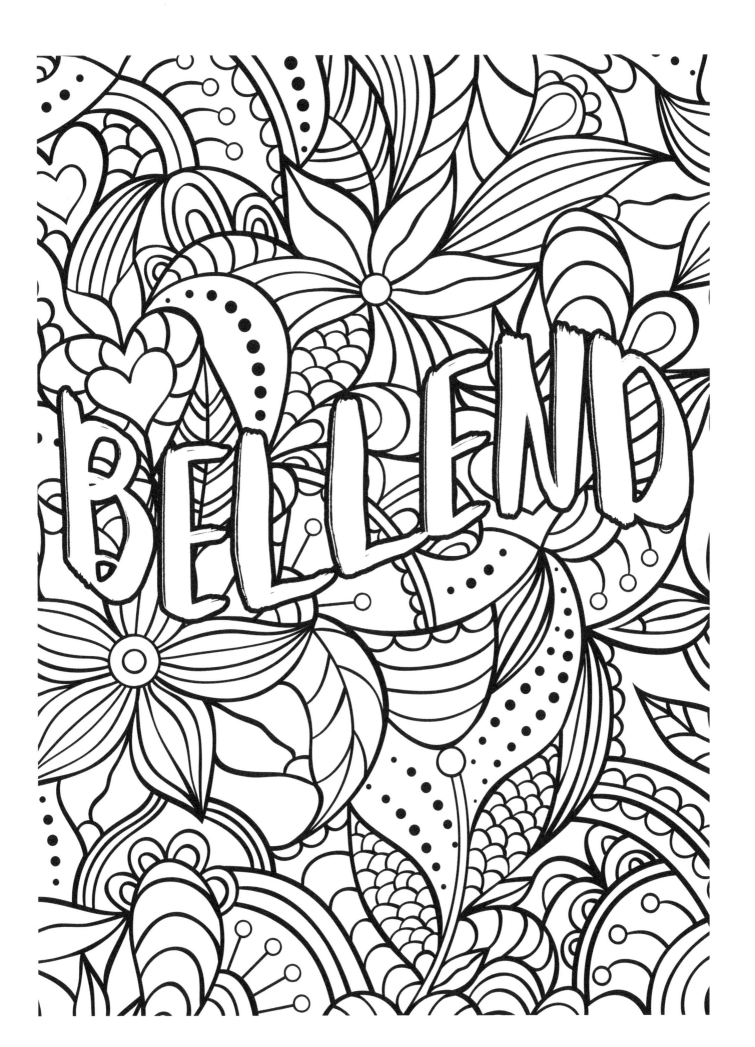

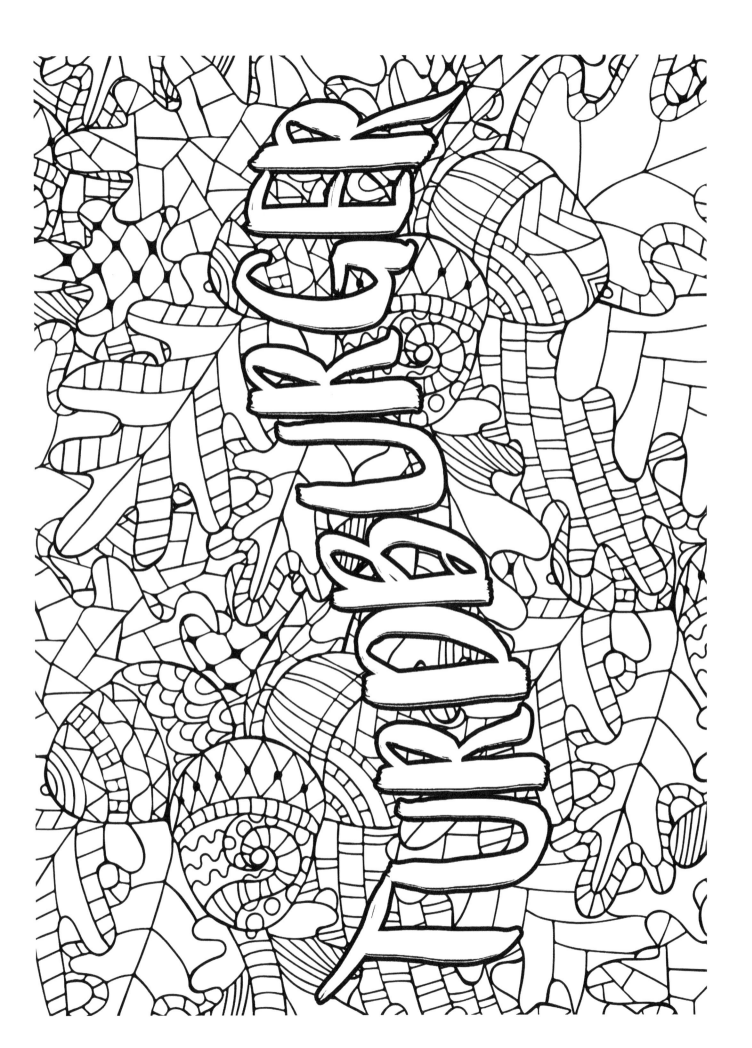

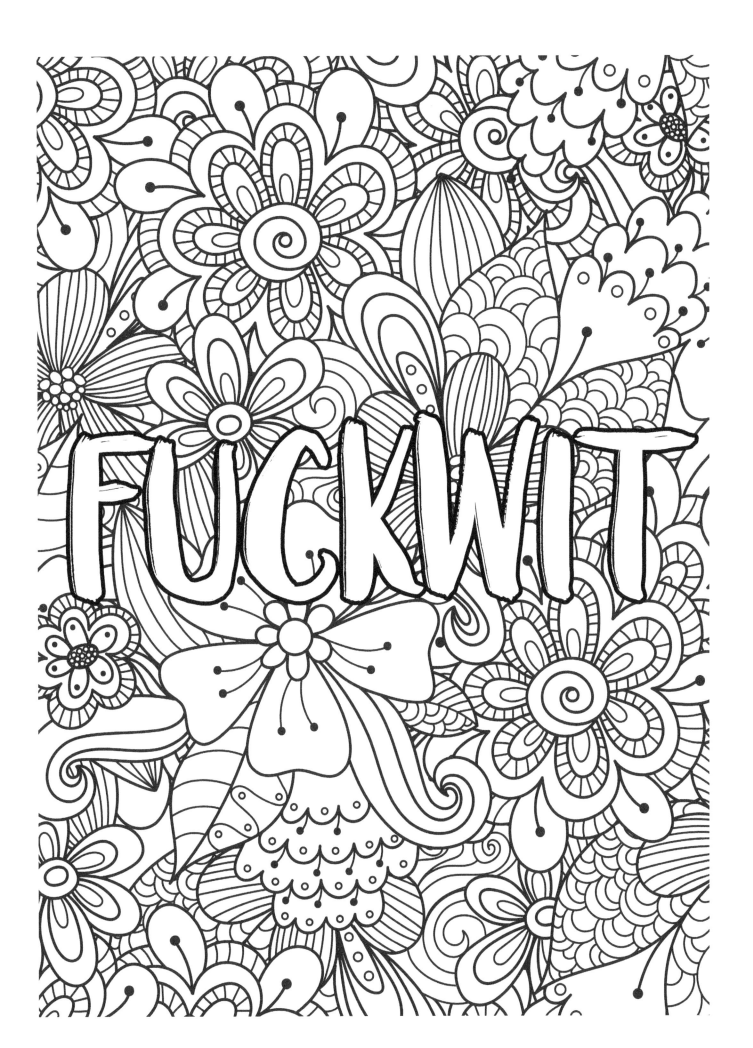

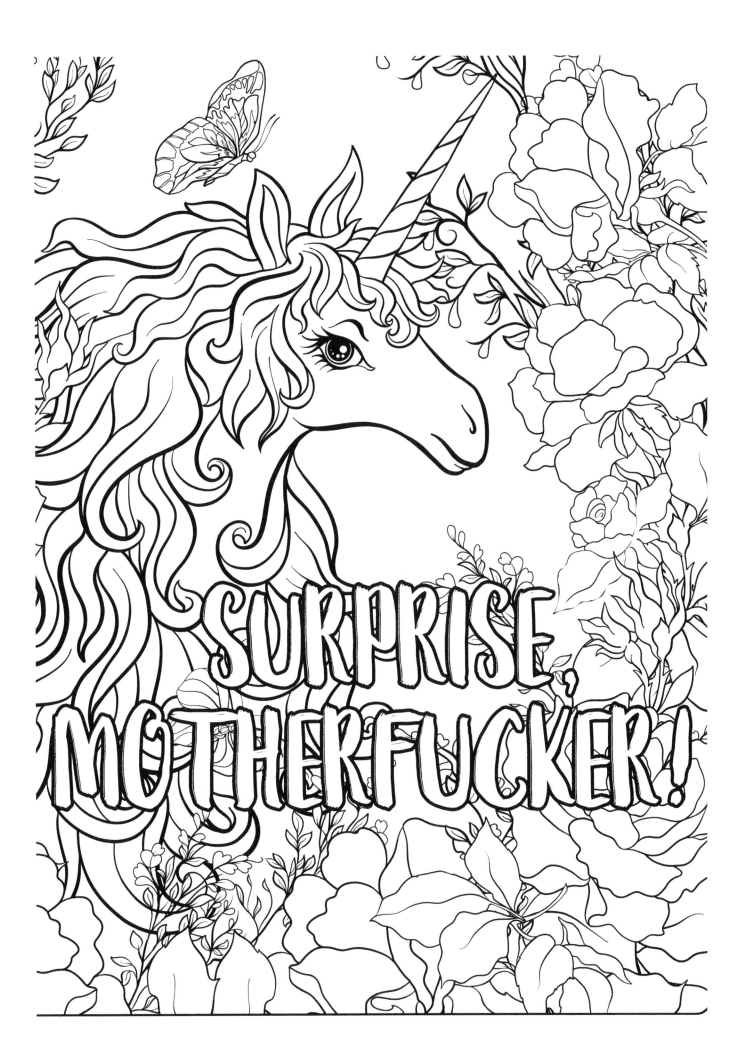

Thanks for colouring! If you would like to discover more adult colouring books in our range, then you can find us on Amazon or at ravensforgebooks.com.

Other titles from Ravensforge Books include:

Shut Up & Colour This Shit: A Swear Word Adult Colouring Book – LEFT HANDED edition
Edited by Georgina Townsend
*

Shut Up & Colour This Shit: A TRAVEL-SIZE Swear Word Adult Colouring
Edited by Georgina Townsend
*

Shut Up & Colour This Shit 2: Insults - A Swear Word Adult Colouring Book
Edited by Georgina Townsend
*

Shut Up & Colour This Shit 2: Insults - A Swear Word Adult Colouring Book – LEFT-HANDED Edition
Edited by Georgina Townsend
*

Shut Up & Colour This Shit 2: Insults – A TRAVEL-SIZED Swear Word Adult Colouring Book
Edited by Georgina Townsend
*

Ocean Dreams: A Nautical-Themed Adult Colouring Book
Edited by Georgina Townsend
*

Dinosaur Days: A Prehistoric-Themed Adult Colouring Book
Edited by Georgina Townsend
*

Ancient Worlds: A Historic-Themed Adult Colouring Book
Edited by Georgina Townsend
*

Country Calm: A Countryside-Themed Adult Colouring Book
Edited by Georgina Townsend
*

Fantasy Magic: A Fantasy-Themed Adult Colouring Book
Edited by Georgina Townsend
*

Cat Capers: A Kitty-Themed Adult Colouring Book
Edited by Georgina Townsend

CPSIA information can be obtained
at www.ICGtesting.com
Printed in the USA
LVHW060955010223
738400LV00010B/187